Facing Faces

A collection of poetry by J. T. Wynn

Facing Faces
Copyright © 2013 by Brown Essence, Inc.

Printed and bound in the United States of America. All rights reserved. No part of this book may be reproduced or transmitted in any form or by any means, electronic or mechanical, including photocopying, recording, or by an information storage and retrieval system- except by a reviewer who may quote brief passages in a review to be printed in a magazine, newspaper, or on the web – without permission in writing from the publisher.

Front cover design illustrated by Ve'Lynncia Morgan.

**BROWN ESSENCE, INC.
P.O. BOX 82462
CONYERS, GA 30013**

Please visit our website at brownessence.com and let us know what you think.

I dedicate this work to the hallow balance God gives all!

— *J. T. Wynn*

Acknowledgements...

I've been roaming earth for only eighteen years now, and I have already been faced with many trials. Through my faith in God I was able to overcome many fears and doubts. To those people who were my rocks my mother – Sonya, Mamma Santos and Little Lee. Those three ladies pushed forth when I didn't believe in myself, and saw the beauty in me, when I was at my lowest.

My Grandma Linda is dear to this piece of work, because her death showed me how truly fragile and important life is.

People who kept me laughing are Rachel, Shannon, and Niko. No matter how much I was determined to hold my head down, they made me smile at the most convenient times.

This first work of mine will be one of many more to come, because God gives me inspiration through everything and everyone. So I take the good with the bad, and roll with the puns. No matter how much older I get, I will never lose sight of how precious words are.

Table of Contents

Mars and Luna… 10
Fire… 11
Struggle bug… 14
Breaks through… 15
Bite me… 18
Dirt in my eyes… 19
That road… 20
Salty tongue… 21
Dirty Mind… 22
Howlin'… 23
Silly talker… 24
Cast away the colors… 25
Car crash… 26
Dreaming baby… 27
Sugar come to me… 28
Tampered mind… 29
Runaway… 31
Sand… 33
Rotting in shame… 35
Being In love… 37

The run…	41
Base line…	44
Made in heaven…	46
Wrapped in us…	47
Louder…	48
Bet…	49
Out…	51
A promise…	54
Tug…	55
The pain I could not explain…	56
Hi…	57
Parachute…	59
He was here…	60
Exposer…	62
Sucker…	66
Naked…	68
Better to do…	72
Skin…	74
Harmless…	75
Goodnight…	76
Puppy love…	78
Worked Too Hard…	79
Who I am…	80
Touch me…	81
The Pain…	82

The heart………………………………………………………83
Swat……………………………………………………………84
Strong…………………………………………………………85
Search…………………………………………………………87
Me………………………………………………………………88
Love is a Lie…………………………………………………89
I'm Yours……………………………………………………91
Try………………………………………………………………92
Disappear……………………………………………………93
Cool as Ice…………………………………………………94
Bottled In……………………………………………………95
Blood Shot…………………………………………………96
A blessing……………………………………………………97
The future needs the Past………………………………98

See...

Do you see what I see?
      what I see...
From miles away
Where our people stay
See the emotion of our culture
          Being washed away
See me?
     I see you
See momma and baby play monkey-see, monkey-do
See daddy and son make a home run and quit the game
See mommy struggling through the snow
Don't know what to do or where to go

Who is you?
     Who am I?
Brother over there sagging his pants to his knees
See sister talking to them boys with her skirt to her waist
See baby just die away?
See brother pull the trigger and
     sister go boom to the ground!
Brother put the gun to his head and down...
     He goes with sister
You see me?
     I see you...
The streets see us on tomorrow's news!

Mars and Luna...

Cold below me
She who holds hearts

Cold below me
He who holds thoughts

Lows before me
She holds questions

Lows before me
He holds another

Air above me
She holds my breath

Air above me
He holds my pulse

Speeding, speeding
Earth before me

We hold hunger for light upon us
To know who will step onto
our Planes
Next!

Fire...

Enter my heart into my soul
        Fire!
        Fire!
Fire, come through...
With these eyes see the sky
        Sky, so blue,
        Blue go pale
Then onto you,
Up one, Two
        Fire!
        Fire!
Oh so hot
Puttin' on the lock for endless clock
        Rhymes I rock:
        heartbeats stop
Birds of a feather fly in flocks
        Higher...
        Higher
Till we reach the top
Run the empire
Long time no see, so flip flop
        I bring the heat
        You bring the beat
Flames grow higher
Long lives love, so love last in us
        Fire go wider,

        Blow into the air
Come back down,
Before the clouds burst into tears
Feel so sweet
        So real,
        So deep
Roaring out to the kids
As they run the streets
Secrets we keep
        Hold on to your rocket
        For you burn out
Ears open listening to your screams,
        Your shouts
        Mommy, daddy we play house
Fuel me up;
I'll fill up to the tippy top
        Words run hot
        The sun's flickering bright
Heat up fast, blazing to the ever lands
Blocking out the past
It's so beautiful, it's so sad
        Fire; fire up, up and away
        This star shine, shooting
Leaving a sign for each life left behind
        Time to time
Fast forward, you can't rewind
Bitter like lemon and lime

Fine as wine

Dreamy as a summer's night
What's left behind is still in sight
Restoring the dust, planting a seed for the rest of us

Fire, fire never burn out
Set on us
Rocket to ear, a bursting in air
Soul locks to trust
Words I speak to restore power in Heaven's creak
Life on earth, we face the concrete
Hard and bleak
The lines of where we stand is a thin streak
Valleys low and mountains steep
The thin line between you and me
Fire running over me
When it rains fire seems cold to me
Spilling over
Stuck in the battle filled
With my feet buried deep
Fire run higher
Now I see

Struggle bug...

Slowly I Crawl
To mountains, so tall

Scared
I ball up inside myself

No balance
I fall free

With legs, so small
There is no log in my way

Before I see the way
Waiting for me to fly away

No love
No love today

Hard pavement, rainy day
Feet over head threatening to squash me

Easy, then I move so fast
You don't know where I am

I'm somewhere near
Where I used to be

Breaks through...

Oh when my heart breaks through
I'll be running home to you
When it falls down
I'll be rolling home
To you
When my heart gets strong
These days will
Be long gone
When the clouds puff up
And the rain falls
I'll be standing
Next to you
When it's said and done
I'll be holding onto you

    DON'T LOOK AWAY
    DON'T LOOK AWAY

I got your love
I got it right here for you
So don't you worry
I got your heart
I got it right here
For you

DON'T LET ME GO
DON'T LET ME GO

I know it hurts
Before it gets any better
We work to make it all better
For me and you

DON'T LET ME GO
DON'T LET ME GO

I know it seems
Like I'm made of steel
But I'm not that strong
I'll be breathless
At the Sound of the gun

FOR REAL
FOR REAL
DON'T LET ME GO

Look at me love
When my heart breaks through
I'll be running home to you

Tell me you care, I see you smiling

Hold onto everything, It's gonna be okay

I got you

    WHEN MY HEART BREAKS

    BREAK AWAY

Bite me...

Let me in first
Off the tracks
Hurry right after
Keep up smoke
Up and out
Of us all
Up we fly
Down we fall
Draw the water
Tides right after
You run after
Up the gates
Into the churches
    Into houses
You come now
I'll watch after
Between the pillars
Seven
Psalm a wander
    Peter fist for He
        Joseph on bent knees
            Come now
              All now

Dirt in my eyes...

Slow steady
    Hard breathing
        Take me to
            The corner store where
                I'll lose my mind
                    Old south
                    Hot fever
                  Dirt in my eyes
                  In my nails
                Sour apples
                Juicy peaches
            Old roads
          Running cold
        Secrets told
    Realty unfolds
    True believers
Dog running
    In us all
        Sleep to
            Feed us all

That road...

Spotty got me swerving

Plotting Burglar with a plan

To hurt her if it gets crazy

The money's gone

Lost it quick

Damn you crazy B....

Objects we're

Physically moving

Salty tongue...

Dry for delivery

Everything taste weird to me

I can't drink anything

Nothing moving me

I'm saying different things

I'm slipping through some where

My heads spinning, I'm shaking in my skin

How's this possible?

A Holy Spirit within

Dirty Mind...

I'm the crazy kind
No I'm the one who's loud inside
          Quiet outside
           Running inside
       Speed walking out
   Crazy thinking kind
 Thinking that would
     Make normal
      Heads explode
   See I have sleepy eyes
      Not the dreamy kind
    Mines dark brown
   You stare into them
  But never figure me out
I save words
You ever heard a monk
       Shout?
   See I lose minds
    I break whatever
  I touch everything too fragile
       I'm the crazy kind

Howlin'...

Right under the sun
       Into the moon
     Then back to you
Breaking into the blindside
        Of every dreamer
The sound of the dead ringer
     Pushing at our body's soul
        Stole my heart Breaker
           Just a pulse racer

Silly talker...

Pop ups on the sky light
      With highlights
           Get your time right

                So it shines right
                  Up to the
                      Point where you

                Turn right
                  Be fine right
                      Define right

                Read the
           Signs right
        So there's
     Nothing left
For wrong

Cast away the colors...

Twenty building tall
Fifty fountain fall
Showing now, here through all
Counting over the wall
The wind with fifty kisses
Press on all
Feet up
Bodies over
Twenty running man
Fifty tumbling man
Bodies start to swim
Bodies fall to float
Under water over into the boat
Fifty bodies old
Twenty bodies young
One body hung
Twenty bursting lungs
What it has become
The world at its end of time

J. T. Wynn

Car crash...

One foot on the brakes
One foot on pedals

Slow down a little
The baby's in the car

Car swerves
Next car comes in fast

Both flip over
That was the nightmare

So be safe here
There's no way

Through a dead end

Dreaming baby...

Caught between smiling
something
Made me
Not screaming
No nightmare can trap me
I'm here
Tucked safely
Running around in circles baby

        And I was there
        And she was there
        You were there

Smiling still, I know I am
It's you maybe
Us together
Pray we never move away from
This place
Just a little longer
In this
Dream world of mine
        With you
        Lost in
        My mind

Sugar come to me...

Pretty flavored
    Cotton ball
Favorite smell
  Heaven sent
Blessing bent
Messing in
My pastry
Making eyes
  No surprise
      Some surprises
         Great maybe
           When they're not
              Hurt I may be
         Maybe sweet
        Like your lips
     Maybe nice
Not so bitter
 Good

Tampered mind...

Buzzed with tainted wine
Soul so blind
Eyes fooled
By design
The way it shine
A gun of hearts
Tearing love apart
One quick shot
For it all to fall apart
Inconceivable parts
This world ready to embark
On with full conception
A loyalty
Our self defense
Has to misconception
Ready, steady
Pressure on
Grab the dart
Before the sound
Moves on
No easy target
Please don't take me

J. T. Wynn

Know me this way...

Take a hold on

    I put my soul on

        Ride far into a war zone

            Trying to find my way home

Don't wanna be alone

    The angels keep me strong

        Pushing cold away from my heart

To keep your heart in mind

    To keep a frame of mind

Runaway...

So sweet, sweet as can BE
                      Make me feel free
Keeping warm with ME
                      You're all I can see
                      Hollow and deep
Same to stay with ME
All we can BE
                      Never let it go
          Take my blood to the river following south
                      Hold this heart close
               As the words we once spoke true
Sky is still BLUE
Peace stay in ME
                      All we are
                      Soon what where
Gonna BE
So why would I RUN AWAY
                      If you're still here
                      I won't run unless
You come with ME
You say go HOME
                      But my home is where….
You are
The only place I wanna BE
RUN AWAY
RUN AWAY

You gonna BE
Running with ME
Run away please
                        Keep safe love
                Find a place and I'll meet you there
            I can't trust they'll let you get to me
RUN AWAY?
                  Why would I runway without you love?
                      I ain't running
Unless you're coming with ME
You say go HOME
                    But my home's
                    Where you are
The only PLACE
I wanna BE

RUN AWAY
RUN AWAY PLEASE!

Sand...

Brand a fan
  A strong hand
Grand pry
    Defy to imply
Or try to hold in place
  Stamina to knowledge
      To theatric
  A show
       For doom
Trace between the lines
     Between the lies
       And tides
  For pride
For a prize
A mile to reach the sun
     That hits the waters
         Onto my feet
That are buried
  Deep in the sand

Astro...

Great lengths
To see stars
For a change
Of cards
To pass
The past by
A make shift of character
Being changed to fit fame
Point a finger at the easiest to blame
Shooting away
For glories grace
Astro for AstroTurf
For Luna and cheese
For sun rays and sunlight
Earth is replenished
Water is refreshed
Eyes are peepholes
To life
Unfold in time
Unfold in us
Bursting into space
Now there's
New meaning to this place

Rotting in shame...

Your eyes are blood shot red. Your voice is cold and draining; your aura is fading and depressing. The words you say are repetitive. Each time you return you come with a new excuse for why you left.

I shake my head and say, "Okay."

I want you to know it's not because I Agree. It's because I have too many things to say and there's just not enough hours in today. Maybe one day I won't have anything left to say. For now, you should know I no longer need your approval to be happy. I cried before, because my daddy left me. I don't cry anymore, because my daddy left me. My tears are too important to waste on your irresponsibility.

I feel so sorry for my daddy, because he's a lost little boy. Who thinks women are toys. He also thinks raising his children is a game. Sorry daddy I'm not your monopoly piece. You can't just move in and out of my life as you please. My heart is real daddy. I felt it when you put a hole in it. I'm okay now daddy the hole is almost gone; so you don't have to worry. I still love you daddy, and always will. I just can't wait for you to grow up any longer.

Every moment you're not in my life my heart just keeps getting stronger. The heat inside of me is burning out; the fire is rained out. I'm moving on with time; I guess that means I'm leaving you behind. Well at least the little boy inside you.

You can't stand behind him forever daddy. Your heart's going to become too heavy for him to carry. One day you won't have any place to put your shame. So, I will pray to God to save my daddy. "God, oh God oh God please save my daddy. Save him before his shame rots him to the core." The little boy will cry so hard his sorrow will create a storm.

It will be heavy and it will rain for days. The little boy will cry and look into the mirror. Then he's going to realize he's not a little boy. He's just a sorry man. Who doesn't know how to be a daddy? Which I don't understand, because all I ever wanted was for my daddy to hold my hand.

I love you daddy

Being In love...

We're always running
We never slow down
You make me nervous
Still I turn around
Your face is bright
Like the sun
I don't want to
Lose out
I don't wanna
Stop now
We've gone for
So long

If you need to
Take me I'll
Figure out
How to be
Stronger
Don't let this
Be the end
Some how
I know we
Can win
It's not too
Late to
Hold on

I'm fighting
As much as
   I can
To be here
  With you
I'm so scared
I've never been
  This scared
    Before

 I want you
But it don't
Seem right
No more
I can't think
  Without
  Your love
So hard to live
  Without
  Your love
It's so hard
Being in love
Being in love
Love takes all
  Of me
So you see
I can't barely

Stand
I can barely
See what I'm
In for
Why is
So much
Just to
Be happy
Just to
Be happy
In love
With love
Love
Love
Love
Being here
With you baby
I'm drowning
I can't breathe
No more
I can't see
No more
What happened?

All I wanted
Was you
Everything else

Came along with
The beauty and
  foreverness
  Can we fight
    It so
We can have it
 Being in love
  In love
  In love
 It's so hard
  So hard
   Being in love

With everything
Weighing us over
 Powering over
  The towers
We're stumbling
    Over
 Being in love
  In love
Love love
One love
  With you

The run...

Am I supposed to run?
   Don't know
   What the hell
   I'm running for
    Why's it taking
     Me so long
      To get to
     The golden door
     How long I've been
      Waiting for
       Running for
      I'll still be going
       When the worlds
        No more
       I've been at it for
        So long
        I jump off
         The floor
        Legs so strong
         I run some more
          Defying gravity
           Holding onto me
          Give me everything
         Give me everything
        Someday you're
        Gonna see

How much it
Takes from me
    Talk to me
Tell me everything
  Tell me everything
    Only you can bring
      The best out of me
        Give it all to me
      Give me everything
      Give me everything
        I hold it up so high
          You can see it now
          Don't take me down
           I won't turn around
            I'll run for more

Till the golden door
Opens up to me
    Opens up to me
How can it be this way?
  So little words to say
      Oh I'm so afraid
        Can you just
          Run to me
        Can you just
          Run to me
      Why does it hurt?
          So bad

Why do I feel?
So sad
Please come
Take my hand
Lift me higher
Please
There's nothing I
Want more
Than that golden door

Base line...

Face mine
Recreate mine
Embrace times like this
Because they're
Hard to find
This heart of mine
Can withstand times like this
It's fine if you don't know
How great this is
Lifeline packed with
What all this is
Be mine
In time you'll know
Why this is
Trace time
You'll see who this is
Sometimes I run to see if I know
Where this is
No fear
No fair
Who cares?
Where time lives!
Face mine
Recreate mine
Embrace time
It's mine

Let me have some
I'm still hungry
For more
They don't sell this in stores
Or on line
So where is
There more
I want more
It's hard enough
There's not much to go around
We get so much
Until our luck runs down
I searched the lost and found
There's nothing
Not for miles around
So hungry
It pounds me down
I'll fake
Wear a happy frown

Made in heaven...

Descended from up above
   A story, a peak
     Of what's there
  Listening for the Truth
What's found in?
   The beauty of youth
    What we look for
As days roll on
  Dreams are bound
   To form
None of that matters
   Unless he calms the storm
    No one will know
How it really is
  It was made
    High above the stars
That's why it's
  Alien to earth
   We only get
A little for so long
  So we won't destroy
    This delicate fabric
Youth was made in Heaven

Wrapped in us...

      Quick to the touch
Looking into your eyes is a plus
  Our fingers locked together
    Gets me all caught up
      Can't see what I like more
        Love or lust
Both are thrills
  That make us bust
Each line as thick as an elephants tusk
        So out of whack
  We're zigzagging across
    The land of "in us we trust"
  And plus God gave us the key
    To the garden of Amor
I'm hiked up on top of the mountains
      Buried in us
Remember the visual
  Of the spiritual plane
        When the light set on us
The more we reminisce
Over this romance
      The more it's wrapped in us
I like the sound of that

J. T. Wynn

Louder...

           Correct me if I'm wrong
              But good things
          Don't usually last long
            The chances are
              Slim to none
    Some try to enjoy the fun
Before the good times are done
Every moment seems forever
Especially when you're young
Playing games like
Ping pong
When it's over the
Last words we say are
Ouch that stung
 The moment breaks
Off piece by piece
You try and grip on
But some how
You're pulled to
Release, but you never really release

J. T. Wynn

Bet...

Waking up to
This world we face
Grasping on to
Life's bitter sweet taste
Trying to keep up with this fast paste
Every girl dressed the same way
All of them covered in lace
Wishing to hold
On to these dreams we chase
Making something
Out of nothing
Precious time we waste
Saying I don't love you when
That's not even the case
Step to me wrong
I'll spray your ass with mace
The government
Feels like we
Middle class commoners
Need to learn our place
To get their attention
We have to say it with a

Little umph, a little base

Don't leave clues
So they can't trace
Although we came
Into this world alone
We all leave with a bet
That the ones who come
After us will make
The same mistakes

Out...

Out to out
Thicker than thin
Blend the ten
Open doors
Flip the fen
    Run me in
    Write this note
    Still not quick to send
    Far out standing up
    Worse thing you could say is tough luck
        Be quick to rush
        Calm down no need to fuss
        Sorry I made you mad
        What you did was F^up
            Down in the dumps
            Sticking it up
            Looking in the mirror
            They're yelling at us
            While saying they love us
                Hold me
                Don't rock the boat
                When times get rough
                Remember the words
                Gandhi and Martin spoke
                # one's best friend is zero

Hold your breath count to ten
You're the biggest hero
Fly away to seize the day
Searching for the right thing to say
Why so serious?
Calm down
Let's play
    Kiss my cheek before we lay in the grass
    I wonder how long
    The good parts will last
    It's time for me to ask you
        Is there something more you would like to do?
        I promised you, sober you
        I would never make a fool of you
        You say you love me
        So act like you do
        Please stay committed
            Another promise I will too
            We roll over
            As our emotions pour over
            The more we know each other
            We never really mean to hurt one another
            The one for me is you
            My best friend, my lover

A guy like no other
Putting 1 +1 together
You and I come out at the end

A promise...

Let's be honest we never planned on keeping this love
You sound like you're the last pea in the pod
Falling over in thick fog
Trying to act twelve feet tall
You can't remember it all
You keep going in circles
Trying to stall
I'm no longer scared to fall
Hoping that this is enough
I wonder which one of us
Will be first to give up
My past has made me
afraid to trust
With my hands faced down
I push off the ground
In my dreams I turn around
Finding myself in your arms
Where I feel safe and sound
If we stay in right now
Then later on figure out
We're better off as friends
I think in all
It will be okay
I'm happy to have known
What it's like to be with you in the end

Tug...

Wash me up
Then watch me dry
Pieces unfold
Behold me,
I come
Here in God's grace
Embrace my journey
I say hear the; hear the
All mighty in me
My soul shall be free
When all is good
The power of He
Bestowed in me
Two Path's pull on me
I shall take thee where
The end is the beginning

The pain I could not explain

It was rushing through
My veins
I was going insane
Everyone said
You can't feel that
My head bursting
In flames
I'm taking a ride
On the crazy train
It thrives where
My heart lives
Wishing that
I could fly
Over mountains
I want to go away
and leave this pain
I won't be a slave
To this pain
That's trying to
Wipe me clean
I just want
To feel joy
And be free

Hi...

Hi, bye
Hello again
I sent letters for a year
I guess
Who we were
Before the great deserter
Made the love disappear
Cold water
Left at the distant alter
Nothing we never thought of
And everything we dreamed to be a part of
I like your new hair cut
You've been working out haven't you
Um I'm just mm
No, you first the feelings between us
Are still so strong
It's like forever and a day
You were gone for too long
Hug me, Kiss me for nights long
When you said
And I was so scared
I'm sorry, Can we start over again

J. T. Wynn

Maybe it's
Just well
I'm seeing
This...
I thought it was over
Don't cry
Just kidding, my love
Of course, we can start over
Hi, I'm time

Parachute...

                No feet can walk in mid air
Well no feet can walk like that
        You would think
                It's possible but no man
        Can make it so
    No one can fly
        But once you get inside
You almost do it
        You can almost
            Fly like you're walking
But you're in a parachute
                It's cool to see
        It from so far Up
            but it seems impossible
It's different
    From a plane
        It's like you're
    So close to defying gravity
    But it's better
        Than nothing
And maybe someday
    You'll find yourself floating in air

J. T. Wynn

He was here...

Unclear unclear
Bloods thick
None shared between
      Us but when
    The future comes
Up a baby is thought of
Youth is so clear in us
Talking about moments
      Laughter unclear
    About moments after
   My chest is keeping
    The heavy beats
    Of my heart in
So I guess my bodies
 Strong enough to keep
      My life still while I take
   Care of the cuts of our love reading the Invisible kiss
You left on my heart , he was here, you're still
      How you stole
      My heart
      And I can
      Feel it beating
      moments after
      X is who you're loving

But you loving
Me is clear
And there's nothing
        After except
        I shed tears
        My anxiety
        Is the letter
        Tilting over
        And I'm still trying
           But it hurts so
        Much I'm dragging
          But your heart
        Would bring me
           Closer to heaven
                7777
        Lips never touched
        Hands never held
        Your heart still
    Stuck on my mind but by my heart
Healing with time but my love its fine I'll keep praying
Someday I'll Have a love that's only mine

Exposer...

Exposer brings us closer
If we could
Break our pride
Oh I broke my
Pride so many times just
To save what's here
But if there was
Nothing here
To begin with
Then I understand
You so close within me
We could be
But it's dumb to me
I've never been so hungry
Your heart
Is a bum to
Me I'd give
You everything
My love can offer
Summer, spring
I love your heat
Circles are so
Dumb to me
But I'll run
If you'll have
Fun with me

If you'll only
Run to me
But not because
I remind you
Of how you two used
To be
If so then
Turn back around
If it's because
You're trying to
Make other people
Happy
Take a look
Around
No one really gives a
Damn about what
We do
And even
If they do
Picture it
Just being me and you
Does your love still
Rain true for me
If we could ever
Get lost in that
I'll tell you
The cost for

That nothing
And everything
Because our
Hearts will
Never feel
Heavier
My love, I hate
Trends so let's break
These barriers
My love is crying
The shadows of
What could be
Are dying
Yet I'm still trying
Your name I am calling
Because I am falling
Hard onto the pavement
You're the only one
Who understands
The language
It's sacred
Don't play
With it
Chasing
Our
Moments
Catching

Our breathing
Feeding our thirstiness
Never forgetting
The reason for it
I'm so cold
Expose me to
Your warmth again
Then hold me
In your arms again
Damn it I'm so
Far so far
So far in
Can you feel me

Sucker...

If you broke me
Then fix me quickly
Please
These birds and bees
Singing
Their words are
So tricky see
Butterflies are
Living proof
The hook to
That one song
With the moment
On that one
Day
You're still stuck
In that he say
She say
But I say
It's time for
Us to play
Nothing else
Matters to me
These words
Flew to me
With our
Emotions glued to me

I promise you
It's new to me, too
But I'm a sucker
What can I say
There wasn't
Enough love in this day
If you were a dog
I'd love to be
The reason why
You strayed
Away from
Home
But I'd keep
You safe and sound
In my heart
You'll have a new home
One perfect for you

Naked...

Never felt so
Never knew I
Was until
You said so
Couldn't notice
Until you touched
The edges of shadow
When you speak
I feel it when
Your words blow
Into the air I'm breathing
I'll shake the snow
Globe of the evenings
That we never spent
You were supposed to
Spend those with her
But her love was lost
For you
We can't change
That but my love
Is new to you
If I'm naked
I never noticed
My heart
Always has been
Open with you

The passion
I have for the
World is something
You share with me
If I'm naked
Be naked too
Maybe our skin's blue
My skin has scars
I know but I never
Noticed because
You never noticed
And if you're not
Breathing
I guess I'm dead
And when it's
Cold I don't
Feel a thing
Exposed is something
I've always been
With you
I could never
Lie to you
Because I could
Never hurt you
But if I'm kicking
And screaming
It's because

You still
Hear me
If you're looking
Like a ghost
My pigment
Would never
Boast cause
If you're naked
I'm naked too
Because if I
Can see you
You said you
See me too
So if we're naked
It's because
God wants us to be
And if it's meant to
Be lasting forever
Melting into
One another
For eternity
Then being naked
Will turn us into three
Or more
Then we could all
Live in our
Wedding rings

But if my heart's broken
Please don't tell me
I'll tell you the
Naked truth
Damn it makes
My stomach
Hurt, heart pound
I'm pretty sure
Love is true
So there's me and you
So naked is how I
Dare to be with you
I have no other
Choice, time is
Losing me
If your love's not
Only mine to have
Then I can't wait
For you
My heart's
Strong
Yes, but
I have to stop
Before it starts
Breaking through
I'm thinking, It's time to put some
Clothes on and you

𝓑etter to do...

Boredom drove
Me to my pj's
Spilt ice-cream
Cups of hot tea
Hot chocolate
Then out the
Door to the
Grocery store
Strolling around
Hands in coat pocket
Penciled in socket
LMN and Hallmark
Channels
Remote glued
To hand
Trying to
Finish
Writing first book
Night ended
With losing
A pen
Right
Before
Lights out
I received a
Call from

A friendly
Friend
Saying
It was only
7pm and
They said
I know you're on
Your
Way to
Sleep
But don't
You have
Something
Better to do
Than sleep
Your life away

Skin...

Slow in the eyes, Need for surprise
Create me with your life, sorrow loves those eyes, but when you
Smile you win it all, No need to cry
Down in the woods, Drunk and dry
My hearts shaking, I don't want to know why I'm so surprised, should have known the lies, you don't know why, so it doesn't matter if you're drunk or dry, your skin Is only telling lies, tie the waters to your mind, flooding inside, makes me feel so drunk, surprise, surprise I'm not even inside
Stop crying to the wind and cursing at the sky, the candy's sweet Our skin sweats so drunk with life Drunk waiting to be revived and if I died I lied to your surprise, so open your soul and close your eyes, I'm the one screaming enter the creation enable good sensations and I don't want to know why, so I cry and cry Hoping that the years will help me hide but in the end it reviled my whole life

Harmless...

The only person I could really hurt is myself, I'd never dare hurt somebody else, I'd never look close to life that the bind I had for them was personal, I mesh when I think about religion and wealth,
It's bursting from sky lines and the very fabric of our connection should have never happened, but I'd always keep you safe with me it's the only thing,
I can offer you even if I'm just passing through and far away these memories will be nothing more than dreams

Goodnight...

Black and tucked
 Back behind
  My traveling mind
   Rush in time with this
    Little line
    Hoping
    For my heart to shine
    I don't
    Want to
     Be so blind
    And hurting
    And I'm cutting my integrity
     I'm delusional
      Maybe illusional
       A little cynical
        Practically
         Impractical
          Broken in my imagination
           Never interment
            For me
             But morning is
              So good to me
               Never intimate
                Only heaven bent

Never making sense
    Gives me possibilities
    I'll still end the day with
    Too many words left
     To say and maybe
        Never feeling satisfied
        Never leaving the past
       Behind and conceiving
The future blindly

Puppy love…

Our innocence so
Obviously caressed
    Our sexuality
        So plainly
Did forever become real?
            So quickly did
        Time mean everything
                As space
              Killed us softly
                So often
              Did we hunt
            Each other's dreams
                  Obvious how
              Clear love could
                Be so blinded
            Did we love to be?
              So desperate for
                Eternity
              So pleasant
            Was the youth
              In our skin
                  Perusing our philosophies
            And fragile was our
        Self esteem
      Until we touched
        And nothing mattered more than us

Worked Too Hard

We've got to stand up for what it really is.
Stop!
We've worked too hard to stop.
We've worked too hard to stop believing.
Our people have died for our rights to just not try.
We've worked too hard for kids not even to make an effort to have knowledge. We've not even got a glimpse of what slaves, our people, our background went through the beatings, taking of culture, the annihilation of the way of life.
All they did just to be treated as all humans should with respect. So many people were held with pain and disrespect.
We've worked too hard.
We've got to stand back up!
The human race….

Who I am...

I am my heart
I am my soul
I am my love
I will fight for my rights
I will not let any
One step on me.
I am beautiful I know who I am: lovely.
I have no shame of me.
I know who I am.
I'm proud to be who I am.
  I am me.

Touch me...

Kisses for Hugs
        A giggle and a blush
          A fist full of tears
          For our love

        A smile full of pleasure
        God making you for me
          You're all the beauty in the
        World
      Oh with everything you say
       And everything you do
         You touch my soul
          Love just
             Touch me

The Pain...

It was rushing through my veins.
I was going insane.
Everyone asked me
How can you feel that?

My head bursting in flames
I'm taking a ride on the
crazy train.
It thrives way deep inside
Wishing
That I could fly.
I want to go away
 And leave this pain.
I won't be a slave
To this pain.
That's trying to
 wipe me clean.
I just want to feel
Good
And be free.

The heart...

I am where the heart is
Filled up then departed
Thoughts are fading and friends are replaced with music
You jumped up and went to the studio
I created a note book full of images
It was so descriptive it made the readers feel like they were in it
I find inspiration where the heart is
Other people stay departed and live life under the pit
Don't get me wrong I love a little funk in my soul sometimes
But I don't need to get involved with violence to find it
When you start understanding and hearing there becomes a silence
It fills the room with embrace and lovers began to chase
And haters give a disappointed face
Feel of soul, heat, and beautiful flows
Through listeners who know where the heart is
Some can't help but dance and make love to the rhythm where they feel the heart is
I knew when I was born to be real you have to have heart
People try to rip me apart and take who I truly am
But they can't because I know where the heart is
Flow!

Swat...

Swat back to be the left...

To be the right
Show no ways swat
No directions just swat
In my face
It's a classic to you
Don't answer my call
Like a far pitch
Swat my ass back
To the no one knows
You don't care to know
No way out No way
too much clutter to think
I threw to the hedge back
No swat no call splat
And everything goes!

Strong...

Strong women
Strong we are all we do.
There would be no one without me or you.
All the pain that we go through
Loving and nurturing
we have to do.
Going through physical pain and emotional roller coasters; I don't think our brothers know all we do, and all we go through.
Strong we are just see and look how far we are.
All the things we do.
Strong we stand
All the power we have
When we go through
Trying is all we can do
We stand strong over and over again
We are the bones that keep the body
Of the world
We teach
We carry loads
We make sure the world stands
We stand strong till the end

Boom Boom
Boom, boom, thump, thump
The rhythm is a blazing

Boom, boom, thump, thump
The way it makes me fill is amazing
Boom, boom, thump, thump
It's so beautiful I'm staring and dazing
Thump, thump, boom, boom
I can fill its flow through my veins
It's driving me insane
It's far from a pain
It's more like a rush
Maybe it's the touch of the rhymes
Or the slowing of time
Whatever it is it's blowing my mind
The sounds of the world
Or recognizing and realizing
With your mind the things you didn't see with your eyes
Boom, boom, thump, thump
Tick tock it never stops
 De we de whap

Search...

Search for whom?
Search for you!
Do you know who?
Do you know you?
Search for us!
Where is us?
Where is unity?
Where is Umoja?
Love me!
Who am I?
Go to school!
Why do I?
Have faith!
In what?

Me...

I am me
Me I will not be a
High school drop out
I will not fall behind in school.

Me I won't fall for the
Boy going girl to girl
Me I won't end up getting
Pregnant with a child I cant
Take care of.
Me I am more than what you see
Me I will go as far as ever to be the best I can.
Me I am me
Can't you see?
I am where the heart and soul of life
 are intertwined.
 Me

Love is a Lie...

So all you that fall will fall forever,
If love was so strong
Why when you're down in the dumps
Love stops holding on,
You want to pick up the tune
When you hear love songs,
What the hell is going on,
If love is so strong what's up with this
War and poverty going on,
Then I open my big brown and realize it's not love
That creates hate
But people twist love
So at the end of the day I'll find myself falling.
Lie to thy soul

A lie that is life
That is life untrue
Thy life brings thy pain
So love it is also a lie
If all is so
Bring me
Thy lie of joy instead of pain

If it is so don't lie of love
I take it so it may be
My heart truth

Life, Love, Hast, Lies
When hate brings pain all I love
Shall not be drained!!!
From my brain the
Idea of love shall be stained
So I don't live a life of shaking, staking pain
I shall not want to die
But neither am I scared of death
Neither is death scared of what is me
Death will not clear my pain
But life will bring me life

I'm Yours...

I'm yours you probably don't believe it
It's too much
For you to receive it
I'm yours something from you to the world
So how could you leave me?
I'm yours and you don't even want
Me
I'm yours and you put a hole
In my heart
I'm yours and when you left it used to tear me apart
I'm yours and I don't even feel
Like you love me
But, now you're not a problem
I'm a great kid
I grow and prosper
You're free and
I don't need to be yours I just need to be me

Try...

      Teaching Them
      Through Thunder
     Throwing tic tacs
     Tripping on Train Tracks
    Tip Toeing Through tuff trails
    Talking on the telephone
    Walking like turtles taking time
    Then again talking to them about this takes Time.

Disappear...

Love is in the air
      People every were
You hear my heart beat
          But once he leaves all of me
Disappears

Cool as Ice...

So laid back
Cool as ice sweeter than lemonade
Fly as birds haven't you heard?
I'm the spice make the hot pepper spice
Just cool that's right
For real all night
Just party and when I walk in the room
Everyone stops and says look at that hottie!
There's always one person you have to tell
"Stop trying to ruin the party"
On that note
Peace to that boy
He's a fine ass shorty.

Bottled In...

Tis the day I weep
But only I do not
I shall not cause
If thy sky is to rain
Someone shall hear

Tis the day I see
Like once before
When all is full inside me
And there's no more room
For more I shall find away
To say something's wrong
Something's wrong
So instead of weeping I write
The words of my soul unspoken
Tis the day I find a way
To still keep it in
With no person to know thy true feelings

Blood Shot...

Blood shot tears filled with all the reasons I can't move on
And all the reasons I despise you
Filled with all the reasons I despise me and you as two in one love
Blood shot tears enough to fill a whole body
They strut down my plush cheeks
They sing an evil tune
No sleeve or tissue big enough to wipe them away
Blood shot tears GO a running down my face
LAUGHING AT MY Despair
KNOCKING MY SOUL BACK AND FORTH
BETWEEN THE LINES I READ AND WHAT I SEE
I already knew would be there
BIG BOLD LETTERS THAT SAY FUCK YOU
NOTHING STRONG ENOUGH TO MASK MY
Aching, BREAKING HEART
BLOOD SHOT TEARS TEAR SO HARD YOU CAN'T TELL
MY PAIN AND JOY APART
RUNNING THROUGH THE CRACKS OF MY VEINS
SCREAMING TO ME YOU'RE CRAZY
IM SCARED
NO I'M AFRAID
NO I'M INSANE
FLESH Boiling OUT IN FLAMES
BLOOD SHOT TEARS ARE RELEASED AND THE DOCTORS
DECLARE ME INSANE

A blessing

My life has been a blessing since the day I was born

Even on the days the tears down my eyes they were pouring

And on the days I felt my life was Flooring

And on the days I didn't want to get up in the morning

And on the days I was pissed through doors I was Storming

And when all my feelings were overflowing keeping me from learning and growing

Hoping each time that in front of others they were never showing

For now I will continue to feel the burning, because there's a hole in my heart forever growing

The future needs the Past...

The future without the past you couldn't take a grasp. Without a mother there is no child. The future of me is the tribute I can give to the world. The future gives me hope to believe there is a better day. The past lets me know I can make a difference. The past lets me know what I do shall never be in vain. They are like my right and left hand, right and left eye, mind and soul. There is no future without the past.

www.ingramcontent.com/pod-product-compliance
Lightning Source LLC
Chambersburg PA
CBHW031411040426
42444CB00005B/514